HOWZAT!

‘ You have to win;
that's what life is all about. ’

Sir Ian MacLaurin
Chairman of the TCCB

First published in Great Britain in 1996 by

Chameleon Books

106 Great Russell Street

London WC1B 3LJ

Copyright for text © DC Publications Ltd

CIP data for this title is available from the British Library

ISBN 0 233 99057 7

Book and jacket design by Jupiter 7 Graphics Ltd

Printed in Spain by Graficas Zamudio Printek, S.A.L.

ACKNOWLEDGEMENTS:
Special thanks to Gaynor Edwards,
Mary Killingworth, Mark Peacock,
Michael Heatley, Chris Green, Rob Foss,
Ian Welch, Paula O'Brien, Edwin Donald,
Tim Hawkins, Angus Miller,
all at Generation Associates,
Adrian Murrell and the guys at Allsport,
all keen cricket fans across the country and the
man who made it all possible - Tim Forrester

Dedicated to

Fairford CC, Gloucs.
Stoke Row CC, Oxon.

David Crowe

Whether you're on your way to another Test century at the Oval or bowling for the pub eleven on the village green, the one thing you can be sure of in cricket is that disaster is never more than the next ball away.

The following collection of cricket anecdotes, stories, trivia and pictures proves that even the world's greatest cricket stars are mortal - and just as capable as anyone else of falling victim to the most embarrassing blunders and gaffes. So even if you think a 'crease' is something your mum puts in your trousers, I hope you'll appreciate this look at the lighter side of cricket.

Mike Gatting O.B.E.

Mike Gatting's writer's fee for this publication was donated to Baby Lifeline, a registered charity, at his request.

Er... team – *yeah*
bats – *yeah*
stumps – *yeah*
grass – *damn!*

FROM HOT ASHES TO COLD SHOULDER

WHEN PLAYERS ARE invited to represent their country, the reply is usually immediate. Unfortunately for George Gunn, still afloat on the euphoria of an Ashes win in Australia in 1912, he forgot to open the envelope he was given containing his next Test engagement and put it in the pocket of his jacket still sealed.

The England selectors, smarting from this supposed rejection, managed to overlook him for the best part of the following two decades until, at the advanced age of 50, he was finally recalled to tour the West Indies in 1929, registering scores of 85 and 47 in his final Test.

> **6 Cricket – a game which the English, not being a spiritual people, have invented to give themselves some conception of eternity. 9**
>
> LORD MANCROFT

SCOTLAND THE BRAVE

SCOTLAND'S INTERNATIONAL goalkeeper Andy Goram admits that, given the choice, he'd rather have wielded the willow wand than donned the keeper's gloves. He's won three cricketing caps for Scotland, and though current boss Walter Smith at Rangers isn't keen on him playing the summer game for fear of injury, he remains a member of Penicuik CC in Edinburgh.

Goram, an all-rounder not a wicket-keeper as you might expect, found himself earning his first cap against the Australian touring side in 1989. The first ball he faced from Merv Hughes turned out to be the moustachio'd one's usual opening gambit – a bouncer. As he prowled back to his mark, ball in hand, Hughes offered Andy some sage advice: 'Stick to football, son!'

TYKE BREARLEY?

MASTER TACTICIAN Mike Brearley was born of Yorkshire stock, but his family moved to London ensuring he would play for Middlesex. Had this not happened and he'd joined the Yorkshire staff, he might well have emulated the likes of Boycott and Hampshire and taken over from Brian Close as captain in 1971.

HEADS OR BAILS?

THE PERFORMANCE OF Papua New Guinea has improved greatly over the years, culminating in their defeat of Canada in 1982. The game was introduced to the country by missionaries in the 19th century as an alternative to head-hunting.

Maybe the Canadians had trouble keeping their minds on the game!

Congratulations Mike, you've been confirmed as skipper against the West Indies.

FRENCH CRICKET

IN 1979, a cricketer was stopped while taking his bat through the French Customs at Calais. He explained what it was used for, but the official was completely baffled by it. He then handed him a list of a thousand items, inviting him to select a suitable category. Eventually, the bat was admitted into France as an 'engine sportif sans movement mécanique', and a duty of 1.25 francs had to be paid.

A Country At War

Down at Fort 15 where they had a large Australian population taken mainly in Greece, they had laid a proper wicket and Test Matches between England and Australia were the weekly showpiece.

Fort 15 was split almost down the middle, with the non-workers from Crete (the Aussies) and the non-workers from the British Army. King Cricket was the one way of satisfying their pretended animosity.

The Germans were completely mystified by cricket and were discouraged from understanding it, especially by the Aussies who took great delight in confusing them. For instance, they informed the 'Unter Offizier' that their slang word for a cricket ball was "bollock". So you can appreciate what it sounded like to a newcomer, hearing for the first time from German lips the words, "You play cricket today, cobber, wiz ze bat and ze bollock!".

SAM KYDD, FOR YOU THE WAR IS OVER

Charity Begins At Home

It's a tradition in Australian cricket for the touring team to play a charity match against a side selected by the current Prime Minister. One such game paired old friends Arthur Morris and Lindsay Hassett, both former Aussie test stars now retired.

As Arthur, who opened for the PM's XI, returned to the dressing room after opening the innings, Hassett asked if he could borrow his bat. He did well, and was later ringed by an admiring throng of youths. The Prime Minister made glowing reference to Hassett's knock in his speech at dinner that night and went on to say, "How typical it was of Lindsay's generosity to give his bat away to one of the small boys in the crowd!"

The Lord's Player

Religion and cricket have often enjoyed a close association, particularly in the days before the Sunday league. Middlesex and England player CT Studd abandoned the first class game to become a missionary — and founded a church in the African jungle whose aisle measured 22 yards, the length of a cricket pitch. In the words of one observer, it "left the Deity no room for a run-up."

Leicestershire and England batsman Albert Knight used to halt the bowler's run-up to offer a prayer to the almighty. Walter Brearley of Lancashire was one bowler who considered this somewhat unsporting, and reported Knight to the MCC!

Mutiny On Tour

"The only difference between Gooch's tour and what happened to Captain Bligh on the *Bounty* was that Bligh got that bit more support from those around him."

Former Australian captain Greg Chappell on England's 1990-91 touring team who lost the Ashes series 3-0.

Major Shock

On an official visit to America, Prime Minister John Major brought with him a cricket bat signed by members of the Test side. On presenting this to his host, President Bush, he explained its significance thus:

"We started playing cricket in England around 1300. The first English XI to play abroad was in the 1850s and when they came to the United States I understand that you beat us. We have not been back..."

Call me a cheat again and I'll smash this silly point over your head.

WISDEN 57 (YEARS) NOT OUT

WHEN THAT DOYEN of cricket writers, EW Swanton, was captured by the Japanese in World War II he, like his fellow prisoners, contributed a book to a primitive library. "When the books began to disintegrate, tattered remnants of gas-cape strengthened the original covers, and rice made a good paste. My chief contribution was a 1939 Wisden which, lovingly rebound several times by skilled men, and having been duly de-bugged and disinfected, is with me still. Marked with the Jap stamp (ie not subversive!), and with the letters AD in pencil before 1939, it claims to be the most-read copy of Wisden ever published!"

WHEN IN ROME...

DURING THE MIDDLE of the 19th Century, Surrey enjoyed the services of a cricketer christened Julius Caesar. The all-rounder who played from 1849 to 1867 always insisted his name was recorded in full in the scorebook wherever he played. He toured North America in 1859 with George Parr's side, represented England with Clarke's All-England XI and toured Australia in 1863-64.

SINK OR SWIM

THE FIRST OFFICIAL tour of England by Australia took place in 1878, but their journey was a long and tiring one which took nearly six months. The spirit on board ship was not always helped by the keen rivalry between states, as was illustrated early on when they sailed through a storm.

Fred Spofforth asked Charles Bannerman, a fine swimmer, what he would do if the ship should be wrecked. "I'll save my brother Alec, then Murdoch, then you," came the reply. When asked about the Victorians, Bannerman said simply: "Let 'em drown!"

Do the Australians still get a big kick out of beating England in an Ashes series?

‘ **We got football, baseball, basketball. You got cricket — baseball on valium.** ’

ROBIN WILLIAMS

TITMUS ON HIS TOE

WHILE ON TOUR with England in Barbados in early 1968, bowler Fred Titmus was injured in a freak accident. As he was pushing a motor boat out to sea, four of the toes on his left foot were cleanly severed — yet he never felt any pain whatsoever.

Because his big toe — the one crucial for balance — remained he was able, with the assistance of a suitably padded boot, to resume his career and in the coming season, just months later, very nearly made the double, scoring 924 runs and taking 111 wickets.

‘Cricket civilizes people and creates good gentlemen. I want everyone to play cricket in Zimbabwe: I want ours to be a nation of Gentlemen. ’

ROBERT MUGABE

England – a happy land we know,
Where follies naturally grow.

CHARLES CHURCHILL 1731-1764

ODE TO A STREAKER

' He ran on in his birthday attire

and sent all the ladies afire

When he came to the stumps he misjudged his jump

Now he sings for the Luton girls' choir! '

POEM SENT TO *TEST MATCH SPECIAL* AFTER A STREAKER INTERRUPTED A TEST MATCH AT LORD'S IN 1975...

' it's the first time I've ever seen two balls coming down the pitch at the same time. '

ENGLAND WICKETKEEPER ALAN KNOTT ON THE SAME INCIDENT...

WRONG-TURN RANDALL

DEREK RANDALL HAD a razor-sharp mind on the pitch but could occasionally be a little absent-minded off it. After a memorable innings against India at Lord's, he left the ground in a good mood and turned left out of the Grace Gates. Setting off towards the Clarendon Court Hotel, his usual place of residence when in the capital, he picked up key number 405 from reception and entered the lift. He was almost at the door of the room when he recalled that he should have been holding the same key at the Westmoreland Hotel, where the England team were in residence...at the other end of St John's Wood!

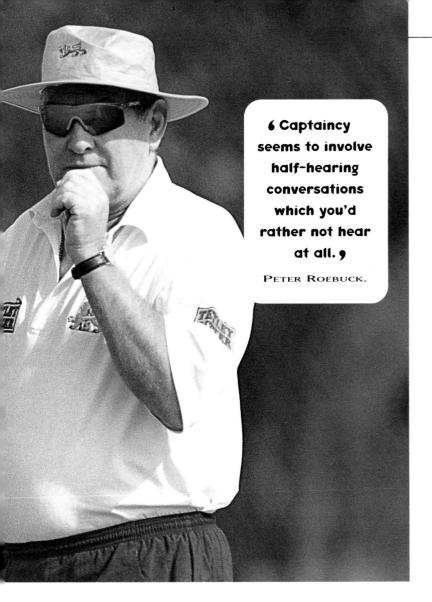

> **6 Captaincy seems to involve half-hearing conversations which you'd rather not hear at all. 9**
>
> PETER ROEBUCK.

A HARD 'DAY-NIGHT'

THOUGH 'DAY-NIGHT' games are an accepted part of modern cricket, there were eyebrows raised back in 1952 when Arsenal FC's Highbury Stadium played host to one of the first games ever played under lights. A respectable 8,000 crowd turned up to witness a benefit for Middlesex's Jack Young played against Arsenal footballers on a matting wicket. Leslie Compton, who could have played for either team, appeared for Arsenal when they scored 189 all out. Curiously, for clubs used to the 11-a-side game, both fielded 13 players.

The Middlesex innings was played under lights with a ball painted white (which was replaced at intervals as the paint chipped off). Even so, Middlesex managed to shade a win, and batted on until 237 all out. Jack Young had appeared at the wicket humorously attired in a miner's lamp!

DOUBLE VISION

ONE ONLY HAS to take a weekend stroll through the parks and playing fields of London to see the popularity of the game of cricket. It is not unusual for there to be as many as ten games being played at the same time in the same park and in such cramped conditions the ball from one match often finds its way onto another pitch.

Such was the case on one summer afternoon when two fielders met under descending balls from two different games. Much to their delight both held their catches safely.

Unfortunately, though, both fielders had managed to catch the wrong ball.

'WILTS'-SHIRE

COUNTIES OCCASIONALLY cross recognised boundaries to play matches, so it was no surprise when Gloucester chose Swindon, strictly speaking in neighbouring Wiltshire, to play a Sunday league game. Unfortunately for them, the groundsman at their chosen ground must have been a rival supporter – because instead of treating the pitch with fertiliser he accidentally dosed it with weedkiller.

CRICKET — THE ENGLISH WAY

THE GAME IS ESSENTIALLY English — and though our countrymen carry it abroad wherever they go, it is difficult to knock it into the foreigner. The Italians are too fat for cricket, the French too thin, the Dutch too dumpy, the Belgians too bilious, the Flemish too flatulent, the East Indians too peppery, the Laplanders too bow-legged, the Swiss too sentimental, the Greeks too lazy, the Egyptians too long in the neck and the Germans too short in the wind.

A good cricketer must have an eye as sharp as a needle, a hand as tough as a thimble and a leg as light as a bodkin. Russia should be able to produce no leather equal to his lungs, and India should not show a rubber half as elastic as his muscles. He should have a frame of iron and his limbs should be as sturdy as lumber. With these qualifications, we may hope to make a foreigner a cricketer.

PUNCH 1888

Testing, testing..... one, two... one two.

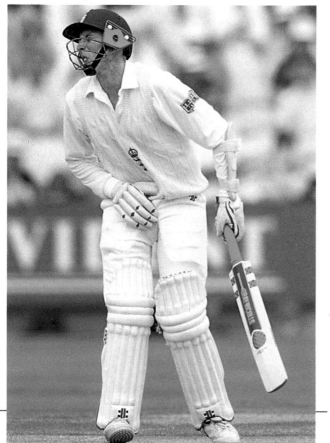

❛ The bowler's Holding, the batsman's Willey. ❜

BBC COMMENTATOR CHRISTOPHER MARTIN-JENKINS DURING A TEST MATCH BETWEEN WEST INDIES V ENGLAND IN 1980-81

AREN'T YOU FORGETTING SOMETHING?

"**ROY VIRGIN** (former Somerset batsman) got about ten yards out onto the pitch before he realised he didn't have his bat with him, so he turned around and returned to the pavilion to get it. This was very embarrassing for him and very amusing for the players and spectators. He eventually rejoined his partner, took guard at the wicket, and promptly shouldered arms to the first ball he received. The inevitable happened; it knocked his off-stump over."

GLENN TURNER

No I bloody won't. It's too hot. Look after it yourself.

MATTERS OF LIFE AND DEATH

THE TRUTH BEHIND THE CAMERA

IN THE DAYS BEFORE air travel between continents became a commonplace reality, newspapers fought to gain exclusives about visiting teams. The *Daily Mail*'s sports editor JL Manning had the bright idea to charter a plane to take the first photo of Australia's side on the deck of the ocean-going liner bringing them to Britain. Reporter Alex Bannister, who was on ship, takes up the story.

"I was to assemble the players at starboard stern at 1.30pm precisely. As the appointed time approached the sea became choppy, there were rain squalls, and the overcoated cricketers became increasingly disenchanted with the project. 'If we had weather like this, we'd give Australia back to the Abbos!' said one through clenched teeth. Suddenly, to my relief, a plane appeared and circled three times at a drunken angle. The picture appearing on the breakfast-tables the next morning was a little out of focus, but no reader was to know that at the moment of crisis the photographer was being violently sick!"

AN EXPLOSIVE SITUATION

"THE BOMB SCARE at Lord's in 1973 halted play for 85 minutes. One or two members who had fallen asleep refused to leave when woken by the police. Umpire 'Dickie' Bird stayed out in the middle perched on the covers along with members of the crowd – but the gates were open for people to leave. The West Indies went back to their hotel – England opted to stay in the pavilion (a lot of good that would have been had a bomb gone off).

"I was on-air when the announcement was made and I continued to broadcast throughout. All the commentators stayed up in the commentary box (which was high on top of the pavilion). We hid our nerves by assuring ourselves that if the bomb did go off we wouldn't have so far to go."

BRIAN JOHNSTON, BBC RADIO

PAT'S PEARLY-WHITES

THE ROLE OF the nightwatchman, a tail-ender elevated through the order to 'see out time' if a wicket falls late in the day, has always taken guts. When Pat Pocock of Surrey was recalled to the England team in 1984 to face the West Indies, he was nominated for the job if either of England's openers should fail against the intimidating attack of Michael Holding, Joel Garner and Malcolm Marshall.

Chris Broad managed to amass just four runs before Garner claimed his wicket — an event that had the England dressing room searching in vain for Pocock. Eventually he was found in the washroom cleaning his teeth. When asked what he was doing, he said: "I was just rinsing out my mouth in case (physio) Bernie Thomas has to give me the kiss of life!"

Ulp, err, yeah, we'll sort this out outside if you want, Devon.

TREE AND OUT

GEORGE PARR WAS a particularly hard-hitting Nottinghamshire batsman who took over the captaincy of the All-England XI when founder William Clarke died in 1856. So strong were his mighty blows to the square-leg boundary that an elm tree growing within the grounds of Trent Bridge was christened "Parr's Tree" due to the many hits it sustained. It survived these, but finally fell in a gale in 1976 – 85 years after Parr himself had passed on.

ON THE SPOT

FREDERICK LOUIS, Prince of Wales and the son of George II, was an early Royal supporter of the game. Sadly his passion was to prove fatal – literally. While playing cricket on the lawn of his Buckinghamshire mansion in 1751, he received a severe blow in the side. Some months later an internal abscess described as 'a collection of matter' burst and instantly killed him.

' Dad? Was there really a three legged, two-headed cricketing creature called a Bothgatt? '

' So legend has it, son. '

' And was it timid, publicity conscious and well-behaved? '

' Don't be so bloody gullible lad. '

WOOD TAKES ROOT

THE REVEREND Elisha Fawcett, c1817, was a Manchester evangelist who devoted his life to teaching the natives of the Admiralty Islands the Commandments of God and the Laws of Cricket. Too poor to purchase a monument to this good man, the parishioners erected his wooden leg upon his grave. In that fertile climate it miraculously took root and for many years provided a beautiful harvest of bats.

DID NOT BAT — DEAD!

KARACHI WICKET-KEEPER Abdul Aziz was the victim of a particularly vicious off-break while batting in the final of 1959's Quaid-in-Azam Trophy. He collapsed and died at the crease while awaiting the next delivery, a tragic state of affairs that resulted in the following score-book entries.

First innings: Abdul Aziz retired hurt — 0
Second innings: Abdul Aziz did not bat — **dead**

AN ENGLAND CRICKETER...

Will NEVER drink alcohol during a match

Will NEVER openly discuss the policy of the Selectors

Will behave with dignity at all times.

ANY WHICH WAY YOU CAN

BROKEN ARM SECURES DRAW

"WHICH TEST PLAYER started his career as a right-hander and finished it as a left-hander?" This was a question jokingly posed by Colin Cowdrey, playing in a game against the West Indies at Lord's in 1963. He feared his future as an England player might be slim after having his left forearm broken by a delivery from the fearsomely fast Wes Hall.

That he returned to the team to captain it was partly due to the courage that saw him return to the wicket, broken limb in plaster, to help save the game and nearly win it. He re-entered the fray with two balls left and England at 228-9 — but never actually had to face a ball, since the previous delivery had ended in a run-out at the bowler's end. Allen, the striker, played out the last two balls rather than test out Cowdrey's left-handed technique and settled for a draw rather than the possibility of a narrow defeat.

PERILS OF PAY OR PLAY

LORD FREDERICK BEAUCLERK combined the roles of cleric and cricketer to unusually profitable effect in the 18th Century. He's reputed never to have made a 'pair', and was so confident of his ability as a batsman that he'd take off his gold watch, place it on the bails, and challenge anyone to knock it off and win it. His yearly winnings through betting on cricket were reckoned at £600 a year — so no need to pass the plate there!

But he was not infallible. He lost the 50 guineas riding on a double-wicket competition pitching him and a bowler called Howard against Messrs Osbaldeston and Lambert. Osbaldeston had retired due to illness, but Beauclerk lost his wicket after Lambert taunted him by bowling wides (which did not at that time count against the bowler). It was sweet revenge for Osbaldeston who, on seeking a postponement, was told "Pay or play" by the greedy cleric.

You're going to say it aren't you? Eh? You're gonna tell me it makes me look a pillock.

A Glovely Moment...

"When a ball is skied near the wicket it's always the wicketkeeper's catch. It went straight up for many a mile. Rodney yelled 'My ball!' and we all stood back and watched him whip his cap off, then run round in a circle as he took off one glove and threw it to the ground.

"Having thrown off one glove, he decided it would be difficult to catch the ball with only one glove so he threw the other one off as well. So there he was with just his inners on — he might as well have had bare hands. After going through another 360 degrees he ended up diving full length without even getting a touch on it."

GLENN TURNER ON FORMER WORCESTERSHIRE WICKETKEEPER RODNEY CASS ATTEMPTING TO TAKE A CATCH

Close Enough!

"I remember playing against Brian Close at Taunton. He was fielding in the stupid mid-off position. I hit one in the middle of the bat and it hit him flush on the shin. My first reaction was to say "Are you alright, Brian?" He replied: "You just get on with your batting. You can't hit the ball hard enough to hurt me, sunshine."

WORCESTER'S GLENN TURNER — SCORER OF ONE HUNDRED CENTURIES — RECALLING THE SUICIDAL FIELDING OF EBULLIENT FORMER ENGLAND AND YORKSHIRE AND SOMERSET PLAYER BRIAN CLOSE

Full Contact Cricket

Defeat looked certain for the Canadians in a match against America in New York, in 1846, when an event took place which certainly wasn't cricket.

The Canadian batsman played a shot straight back at the bowler and, upon realising that he was about to be caught out, decided to tackle the American. The bowler was sent crashing to the floor but managed to keep hold of the ball which he then hurled at the batsman, delivering a blow to the Canadian's leg.

After being given out by the umpire, the batsman returned to the pavilion with his partner. The Canadians did not return to the field and the match was awarded to the Americans.

Afterwards, the batsman claimed that he was not breaking any of the rules of the game.

THANKLESS TASKS

"ALL MATCHES HAVE one thing in common. You will go home with a headache. When I get to the ground there is always a member waiting for me. There is a good chance he will want to complain and that complaint will have nothing to do with my job. It may be: (a) Why did Fletcher declare against Middlesex and lose by two wickets? (b) Why isn't Ian Lilley in the side? and (c) Did I know that beer was 2p cheaper in Bristol, Chesterfield and Southampton?

"It was none of these today. He wants to know why he couldn't get his car in at Worcester and wants to instigate a reciprocal arrangement against any visiting supporters from the Midlands."

PETER EDWARDS (FORMER GENERAL MANAGER OF ESSEX CCC) ON THE HASSLES OF BEING A COUNTY SECRETARY...

TAXI!

ALTHOUGH WG GRACE was never a professional, it must be said that he did make a fair amount of money out of the game of cricket and would regularly arrive at the MCC by taxi and refer the driver to the club secretary for payment of his fare.

On one such occasion the secretary, tired of these insistances, told the driver to seek payment from Grace. He found him in the changing-room in a state of undress and relayed the message from the secretary. His reply was to get dressed, get back in the taxi and return home. It is said that the MCC never questioned Grace's taxi fares again.

YELLOW PERIL

"A BODY OF THE unfit, elected by the unwilling, to do the unnecessary. A committee is like bunch of bananas. They start green, go yellow and in the end there isn't a straight one in the bunch."

FORMER WARWICKSHIRE SECRETARY LESLIE DEAKINS ON CRICKET COMMITTEES

TOP NOTCH

"It won't stop it from going grey. Indeed if it goes really grey I might become chairman of the England selectors."

FORMER ENGLAND CAPTAIN GRAHAM GOOCH
ON HIS NEW HAIR GRAFT

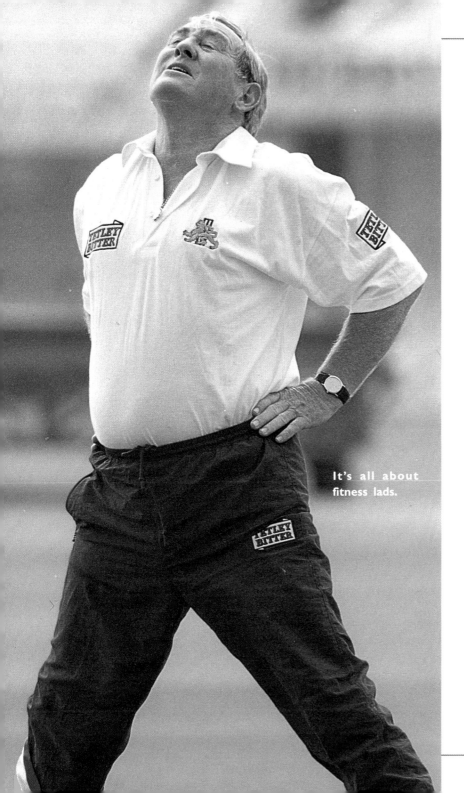

It's all about fitness lads.

6 The captain of a county cricket team is, all at once, a managing director, union leader and pit-face worker. He has almost total charge of the daily running of the concern: he is the main, if not the only, representative of the workforce in the boardroom (ie on the committee), and he has to field, bat and maybe bowl. He conducts the orchestra and he performs: perhaps on the front deck of the violins or as second tambourine (it varies: I've been both). Consequently it is hard to play God, to read the Riot Act about carelessness or incompetence, when one's thrown one's own wicket away or played ineptly – if not today, 9 tomorrow or yesterday.

MIKE BREARLEY

BOUNCERS

DUCK!

WITH THE POWER of some of today's fast bowlers it is not surprising that many batsman are taking to the field looking like ice-hockey players in an attempt to avoid injury from an over-zealous "bouncer".

One only has to remember England's Fourth Test Match against the West Indies in 1995 and the damage that a ball from Kenny Benjamin did to Robin Smith's face to see the prudence in such action. Smith was left with a broken cheekbone which required surgery and he played no further part in that season's cricket. Despite this, there has only been one fatality as a result of being hit by the ball in English first-class cricket.

This happened in 1870 when George Summers was hit on the head by a ball from JTBD Platts during a match between Nottinghamshire and MCC. After this incident, Summers returned to his home in Nottingham where, unfortunately, he died four days later.

Get outta here man... you're too damn short to be a West Indian bowler.

PICKPOCKETS...

HOW
ZAT!

MOSQUITOES...

GREEN GOVER HIT FOR SIX

WHEN MIDDLESEX entertained Surrey at Lord's in 1929, onlookers were touched to see the experienced veteran Patsy Hendren take opposition new boy Alf Gover aside for a few friendly words before the game. He hoped Alf would enjoy his game at cricket's headquarters, and hoped he wouldn't pitch anything too short at him when he came in to bat as he couldn't pick up the ball too quickly these days, being of advanced age.

The youngster recalled these words as soon as Hendren reached the crease, and bowled him a series of bouncers — all of which were duly dispatched over the boundary ropes. At the end of the over, Surrey's Jack Hobbs enquired what the youngster was trying to do. "Oh," came the reply, "Mr Hendren doesn't like short bowling these days. He's told me himself..."

DO YOU LIKE SHORTS?

"IT'S RUBBISH TO say I started the intimidation thing by asking him to bowl bouncers. He wasn't bowling bouncers. He was getting the ball to rise off a length. After he'd been warned for supposedly bowling one bouncer he banged the next one in really short and it flew over our keeper's head. He turned to the umpire and said: 'Now *that*'s a bouncer.'"

FORMER ENGLAND CAPTAIN RAY ILLINGWORTH ON JOHN SNOW'S SHORT PITCHED BOWLING WHEN ENGLAND WON THE ASHES IN AUSTRALIA IN 1970-71

PERFECTLY JUDGED

"ROBIN ONLY EVER pulls his head out the way at the last split-second. He loves looking down the gun barrel. He does it just for the buzz. He is one of the bravest people I've ever met. Probably the only batsman in the world who loves fast bowling. The faster the better. Some are good at playing it, but Robin is actually turned on by it."

EX-ENGLAND AND HAMPSHIRE OPENER CHRIS SMITH TAKING ABOUT HIS BROTHER ROBIN'S LOVE OF FACING FAST BOWLING

BLOW BY BLOW

"WE USED TO play on uncovered wickets without helmets. I never had any fear because I was playing against fully grown men when I was eleven and professional footballers at Bradford Park Avenue when I was fourteen. That's when I learned that you only went out onto the pitch with one thing that mattered — winning. Cricket is only played with soft balls really. The only balls which hit me were short-of-a-length ones — not bouncers. I took my hands away and accepted the blows on the head or the body. These days players get hit on the hands and arms. That's bad batting."

FORMER YORKSHIRE AND ENGLAND CAPTAIN BRIAN CLOSE ON CRICKET HELMETS

HOW
ZAT

For God's sake, you can't all want to go to the toilet.

CRICKET: THE SPORT OF DUKES AND GENTLEMEN

THE DUKE OF EDINBURGH is not often considered to be a cricketing character, but he's long been an enthusiast. In 1949, after he was nominated President of the MCC, he played in a game at Hampshire's Dean Court, Bournemouth ground and, despite his experience running only to captaining his school XI at Gordonstoun and a few naval games, acquitted himself well with a wicket and 12 runs. "The Duke, wearing an I Zingari cap, came in at 191 for 5," reported the *Daily Telegraph*, "and, beginning with a straight drive for two brought the crowd to its feet with two fine crisp drives past mid-off for four, all along the ground. He stayed long enough to suggest that he would hold his own in the company of good cricketers... if only he had the time to practice!"

The Duke was also present at Trent Bridge in 1964 to witness an act of sportsmanship. Boycott hit Hawke to mid-on, and the batsmen ran a quick single. But the bowler, in diving for the ball, knocked Titmus over from behind as he ran towards the striker's end. Titmus was well out of his ground when Australian wicket-keeper Wally Grout received the throw, but he let the batsmen complete the single. Colin Cowdrey, watching from the dressing room, acclaimed this later as "a marvellous example of the true spirit of cricket — he paused for a moment with his hand over the wicket, then threw the ball back to the bowler without removing the bails."

Yeah, an then we'll tell the Press we're too stressed and shagged out to have won anyway.

OFF WITH HIS BAILS!

CRICKET IS WATCHED and played by people from all walks of life and in 1991 HRH the Prince of Wales showed that even royalty can't resist the feel of the willow bat and the call of the crease.

At the opening of an indoor school for the Arundel Castle Cricket Foundation he scored a respectable four not out off four balls from the bowling of 11 year old Luke MacDonald.

This had not been the Prince's highest total as in 1968 he had managed 20 while playing for Lord Brabourne's XI in a charity match against a Grand Prix drivers' side in Kent. Charles' innings, which included two fours and a six, came to an end when he was caught by Bruce MacLaren off a ball from Graham Hill.

Commentator Raymond Baxter observed: "Charles has scored two so far. Oh, I'm terribly sorry, that should be six. Chaps have been put in the Bloody Tower for less."

Yes, Ian, they're 335 for two, Yes, Richards is on 211, and yes, I want you to bowl into the wind.

Yay! Now it's my turn to lose a Series.

HOWE'S THAT, MAGGIE?

FORMER CHANCELLOR Geoffrey Howe's resignation speech on 13 November 1990 contained one of the most widely quoted cricketing metaphors of all time when describing the thankless task of serving under Prime Minister Margaret Thatcher. "It's rather like sending in your opening batsmen to the crease only to find the moment the first balls are bowled that their bats have been broken before the game by the team captain."

CLOUGH ON CRICKET

"CRICKET WAS MY first love. I would gladly have swapped the dream of a winning goal at Wembley for a century against the Australians at Lord's. I have the greatest respect for Geoffrey Boycott. I still take delight in reminding him of the day I got him out, caught-and-bowled, at Lord's in a charity match. He will say he spooned it back deliberately — don't you believe it. He couldn't read my wrong-'un."

BRIAN CLOUGH ON HIS YORKSHIRE HEROES

B.B.W.

The historic moment in 1993 when Steve Waugh shattered Rod Marsh's record for sinking 32 cans consecutively while upside down during a County match.

HOW ZAT!

Merv Hughes prepares to open the bowling in the second test at Lords.

But it didn't affect the results.

RAIN STOPS PLAY

IT NEVER RAINS, BUT IT POURS...

BRITISH SUMMERTIME is notoriously opposed to outdoor sport but it would seem that it has taken a particular dislike to Australian and Hampshire cricket.

Only three Test Matches have been abandoned in England because of the weather without a ball being bowled and these have all been against Australia.

Hampshire is another team that Mother Nature obviously doesn't support as their chances of winning the County Championship title for a second year running were hampered by bad weather.

The side, which had seemed destined to win the title, had their last game rained off and have never won the Championship since.

The weather must be a Worcestershire supporter as they went on to win the league, leaving Hampshire in second place!

SUNDAY DRIVERS!

TRAFFIC STOPPED PLAY is an unusual headline — but it happened in June 1963 when Middlesex's match with home team Kent was delayed when only three of their side turned up. The rest had spent Sunday in the Capital after starting the game on Saturday. Grid-locked traffic in the Tunbridge Wells area meant that they were all still on the road at the scheduled start time of 11.30am.

The umpires declared Middlesex's first innings closed, and Kent captain Colin Cowdrey lent the visitors eight players to make up the numbers. As more Middlesex men arrived, only five were needed — one of whom, Prodger, took a catch in the same innings in which he'd also scored a half-century! In the event, rain prevented a result in this most peculiar of matches.

PUDDLES ON THE PITCH?

WAYNE RADCLIFFE, a local league cricketer, was banned for five years by the Wakefield and District Cricket Union for urinating on the pitch. "By the time a wicket fell I was desperate," he later pleaded. "I turned towards some trees and answered a call of nature. I didn't think anyone saw me."

For God's sake lads, there's more than one box in the bag.

'It looked great, but you're
still bloody out, Derek.'

BIG HITTERS!

THE BASHER OF BUXTON

CLIVE LLOYD IS NO respecter of bowling attacks, whether captaining the West Indies or his adopted county Lancashire. One Saturday in June 1975 he was in Buxton in a game that had been interrupted by snow. Eye-witnesses might have thought that a strange enough occurrence in an English summer, but more was to come. As a weakened Derbyshire attack trundled in, the ball began passing the boundary with rapidity.

The *Sunday Times* reporter Richard Streeton had been ringing in his tea-time report as Lloyd's assault reached its peak, and he concluded it with the wary warning: "I'm afraid you will have to take a re-write later on. While I have been giving you this copy Clive Lloyd has hit eight sixes." Along with the 11 Derby players he was, perhaps, the only man in the ground to be praying for more snow!

Lloyd made 167 not out, his 'ton' coming in 130 minutes.

(£)100-1 SHOT

TREVOR BAILEY'S stubbornness at the crease was legendary — never more so than when in 1953 he occupied the crease for four and a quarter hours at Lord's to save England from defeat against the Australians. He beat even that record when he took over seven and a half hours to score 48, again against the Australians, in 1958. The same Brisbane ground four years earlier had seen him score a six which went right out of the ground. The incentive on that occasion was a local businessman who offered £100 to the first player to clear the boundary ropes. The money — a good deal in those days — was spent on a party for the England team at their hotel; but the odds on Bailey being the benefactor must have been long indeed!

HIGH-HOPES

DURING HIS innings in a county match, WG Grace lofted a ball high into the outfield. He began to run and, as he turned to make his second, saw a fielder position himself under the ball. With quick thinking, he immediately declared the innings and avoided being given out on the grounds that the catch had been taken after the close of play.

CANTERBURY TALE

CB FRY ONCE caused a furore during Canterbury week at Kent when he complained that the bowler had been tossing the ball into the sun. He made an appeal "on two grounds — against the light and for unfair play" — and, when the crowd complained as he left the field, stood at the pavilion gate and declared: "Very well. I shall now bat all day tomorrow."

He didn't quite carry out his threat, but by making 112 in addition to a first-innings 123 he saved the match and, in so doing, deprived Kent of their third successive championship.

BEEFY OUTGUNNED BY GRAEME

IAN BOTHAM'S eventful career took yet another turn in May 1988 when he returned to Taunton, scene of some of his greatest performances when playing for Somerset, in the employ of his new county, Worcester. Many of the spectators had flocked to see their former hero, still bright in their memories, but ended up watching 21-year old Zimbabwean Graeme Hick run up a score of 405 not out.

In nine and a quarter hours Hick — who'd go on to play for England after qualifying by residence — faced just 469 balls, and his boundaries totalled 35 fours and 11 sixes. Somerset batted twice but could still not exceed Worcester's 628-7. Although Botham bowled in both innings, he failed to record a wicket against his former team-mates.

It's all right. I think the umpire's family has gone now Mr Gatting.

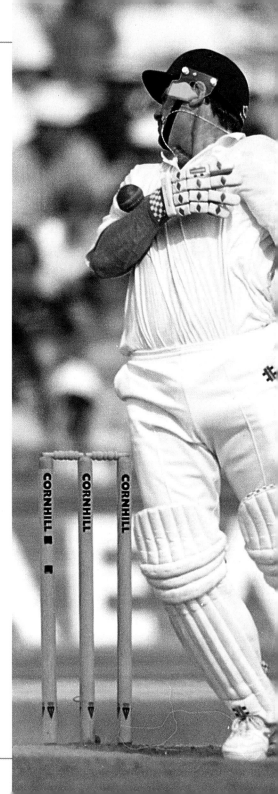

EXTRAS

A SLIP OF THE TONGUE

THOUGH NOTTINGHAM and England's Derek Randall was one of Test cricket's finest cover fielders, he was also prone to the occasional wild throw. During Australia's second innings at Adelaide in 1981-82, he managed to create overthrows with a particularly wayward return, causing Chris Tavaré in the slips to remark to Eddie Hemmings, "He's just thrown that ball for more runs than we've made in the whole match!"

YOU NEED RUNS TO END BAD RUNS

MANY TEAMS ENDURE bad runs from time to time — but Northampton's victory against Leicestershire in May 1939 signalled the end of a four-year wait for a County Championship win. A total of 101 games had elapsed since their last victory, while it was their first win at their own County Ground for six years and their first in the county since 1934.

As luck would have it, war intervened before they could prove beyond question that their form had indeed turned the corner. Their long-suffering supporters would have to wait until July 1946 for their next County Championship success.

LOOK — BOTH HANDS!

THE THEATRE OF THE Absurd, starring the genial Ed Giddins, was pulling them in with the recapitulation of Thursday's astonishing no-ball called by square-leg umpire John Harris. The rumbling controversy was not so much whether or not his delivery to Aftab Habib was illegal (all agreed that it was) but how and how often it was perpetrated.

Giddins declined to explain the motive or demonstrate the method, but the prevailing consensus insists that the ball was transferred from the right hand to left in the delivery stride and projected towards the astonished batsman while the right arm was still in a delivery arc.

DAILY TELEGRAPH, JULY 1996

> ❛ He played his cricket on the heath,
> The pitch was full of bumps,
> A fast ball hit him in the teeth
> The dentist drew the stumps. ❜
>
> ANON.

> ❛ An umpire
> should be a man.
> They are for the
> most part old
> women. ❜
>
> ROBERT FITZGERALD.

Oy! Back in the dressing room you lot: it's not England's turn to bat yet.

QUACK, QUACK, OOPS!

DON'S DISASTER

AN HISTORIC EVENT took place on 14 August 1948 when, at just before six o'clock in the evening, Don Bradman came to the wicket to play his last ever Test innings. He needed just four runs to make his Test average exactly 100, and the crowd and players alike cheered him all the way to the wicket.

The first ball from Hollies was played back to the bowler, but the second, a googly, took the inside edge of the bat and broke his wicket. He had been bowled for 0.

An interesting aside to this was that the TV camera crew had caught Bradman's dismissal, but not Hollies delivering the fatal ball. So they went back and spliced an earlier delivery together with the wicket, little realising he was bowling round the wicket and not over it as he did to the Don.

CELEBRITY QUACKERS

MANY A FAMOUS name has started his first-class career with a duck – in some cases, several of them in a row! Len Hutton scored zero for his first game for Yorkshire Seconds, a duck in 1934 for the firsts at Fenner's and a duck in his first innings for England against New Zealand. Others who failed to trouble the scorers first time out include Wally Hammond, Tom Graveney, MJK Smith, Norman Yardley and David Sheppard.

HEAR NO BALL, SEE NO BALL...

THE BY-PLAY BETWEEN spinners Fred Titmus (Middlesex) and Pat 'Percy' Pocock (Surrey) was legendary. When the notoriously hard of hearing Pocock arrived at the crease to bat, Titmus noticed he was wearing glasses and when he asked the reason, was told they were "To hear the ball better".

The first ball from Titmus was enough to clean bowl the bespectacled tail-ender who, on passing his 'assassin' en route to the pavilion, was told "Well, you didn't hear that one very well, did you?"

WAITER, THERE'S A FLY...

PERCY'S PREDICAMENT

AT LORD'S IN 1930, England's chances of saving the game when Don Bradman led the Australians to a massive 729 rested fairly and squarely with captain Percy Chapman and Gubby Allen. Their partnership of 125 seemed to have all the makings of a cricketing lifeline — until someone spotted a fly in the ointment.

More literally, the fly was in Chapman's throat, having flown unnoticed into his mouth and been swallowed. Still in some discomfort, he was caught behind having made 121... and with him went the home team's chances. Australia followed up with another win to regain the Ashes and 'fly' home victorious.

❛ **I do love cricket, it's so very English!** ❜

ACTRESS SARAH BERNHARDT
— WHILE WATCHING A GAME
OF FOOTBALL

Eh? No, I don't want to play for England.

> **❝ I thought he was going to dive and decapitate himself — badly. ❞**
>
> MIKE HENDRICK BBC-TV

> **❝ Bill Frindall has done a bit of mental arithmetic with a calculator. ❞**
>
> JOHN ARLOTT BBC RADIO

> **❝ Henry Horton's got a funny sort of stance. it looks like he's shitting on a sooting stick. ❞**
>
> BRIAN JOHNSTON, BBC RADIO

> **❝ Strangely, in slow-motion replay, the ball seemed to hang in the air even longer. ❞**
>
> DAVID ACFIELD BBC-TV

A bottle of Champagne will be awarded to the funniest non-sexist caption offered to this picture.

All references to maidens, bouncers, sticky wickets and/or the crease are banned.

The prize winner will also have his or her caption used on any forthcoming reprints of this book.

Until a suitable non-sexist Nineties-style caption can be found, the publishers have settled for:

'Excuse me Miss.... the lads wondered if you'd consider opening for Australia?'

LOUD CROWD

BRIAN DAVISON, the Rhodesia and Leicestershire batsman was coming in for some particularly virulent criticism on a visit to Yorkshire. "Get back to South Africa," yelled a spectator. "We don't want your kind here." He bore it all with good spirit, but when he dropped a catch the remark that followed – "Told you you were no good. Get back to bloody Rhodesia" – proved the last straw. He disappeared into the crowd, determined to make his point to the loudmouth. Everyone's gaze went with him, including that of wicket-keeper Mick Norman – who had cause to regret it!

Ever the professional, Davison had made sure to return the ball before he made his unscheduled 'excursion', and a pinpoint throw cracked the keeper on the knee. While he rolled around on the wicket in obvious agony, Davidson sorted out his differences with the 'gentleman' in the crowd.

SAY THAT AGAIN...

JOURNALIST TIM HEALD overheard the following conversation in the supporters' bar at Bristol:

"Someone ordered a pint of 'lunatic soup' and explained, 'Cider, that is'; another man came in and said 'Who needs Lawrence with an Irishman like that Curran in the side?', and the man behind the bar said, 'He's not Irish, his dad's from Ceylon and he's from Zimbabwe,' and the earlier speaker said, ''e got an Irish passport, 'e wouldn't be playing for us if 'e wasn't Irish.' Someone else observed that if he had an Irish passport he must be eligible to play for England..."

SHORT-SIGHTED SO'N'SO

NORTHANTS TOOK the field at Scarborough in 1981 to play Yorkshire in the middle of a furore. Ray Illingworth had suspended the crowd's favourite, Geoffrey Boycott, for remarks made to the press, thereby evening the odds somewhat, but home spectators were less than amused. As Geoff Cook led his men through the crowds to the field of play, one rounded on Allan Lamb and declared: "As for you, you've no bloody right to be here at all. Get back to South Africa!" Unknown to him, though, the player he was lambasting was Tim Lamb, the younger son of Lord Rochester. Allan was elsewhere.

RELIGIOUS RECEPTION

THE BISHOP OF Ludlow, the Right Reverend John Saxbee, often wears a baseball cap with a radio fitted inside to keep up with cricket commentaries. "At a meeting of rural deans," he revealed, "I was obliged to wear the cap throughout so that I could keep everyone informed on how the Test Match was going!"

Hey Lads, when our wives see us on telly I bet they think we're really cool...

BAILEY'S BOIL

TREVOR BAILEY, the England bowler who's been a part of the BBC Radio Test Match Special team for so long, will forever be known as 'Boil'. The name was inevitably given him by the late, great, Brian Johnston but was derived not from his cricketing ability or even his appearance.

In the days when summer and winter sportsmen abounded, Trevor used to play cricket for Essex and football for non-League Leytonstone. It was a supporter of that club, situated in the East End of London, who unwittingly gave the great man his new name when he yelled in broad cockney: "Come on, Boily!"

A FAIR CATCH?

IN 1924, PATSY HENDREN was touring Australia in Arthur Gilligan's team and during one match was fielding in the deep under Sydney's famous Hill. A batsman made a towering hit, and Hendren moved to get into position for the catch. As he did so, and an eerie silence reigned, a spectator's voice could clearly be heard: "If you drop that catch, Patsy, you can sleep with my sister!"

When later asked why he took the catch, he explained: "I hadn't seen his sister!"

In adherence with the understated traditions of the game, England fans were able to merge with the local crowds in South Africa with barely a discernible sign of their presence.

THE PROBLEMS OF TOURING ABROAD VOL. II

Dressing rooms on the sub-continent often differ from standards English players have come to accept as the norm.

Local catering arrangements can guarantee plenty of runs.

HOW

His Grace Of Gloucester

When the sixties saw your rise
  WG

Cheers were mingled with surprise
  WG

Time it seems has made some blunder,

Still the plaudits sound like thunder,

We've forgotten how to wonder
  WG

Though a generation's gone
  WG

Full of honours you go on
  WG

Honours gained or grudged by no man,

For you've made, from Daft to Lohmann,

Made a friend of every foeman
  WG

Now the hundredth hundred's up
  WG

You have filled the bowler's cup
  WG

You have filled his cup with sorrow

Solace be of Hope can't borrow

For you'll do't again tomorrow
  WG

Stay of Gloucester, England's pride
  WG

And of all the world beside
  WG

Fame soon yours, you've never lost her;

Now, the game of games to foster

We acclaim Your Grace of Gloucester
  WG!

POEM WRITTEN TO CELEBRATE WG GRACE'S CENTURY OF CENTURIES, RECORDED AGAINST SOMERSET IN MAY 1895

HERO WORSHIP

IN THEIR OWN WRITE

"**AUTOGRAPH COLLECTING** is all about physical contact with the idols of our youth. I shall never forget Robin Hobbs coming down the pavilion steps at Chesterfield with a beer glass in one hand and a fountain pen in the other saying to a group of apprehensive youngsters: 'I'm ready for you now.' I once watched my son, then seven, chase Jim Laker up six flights of stairs to be rewarded at the top in recognition of perseverance and exhaustion.

"Those pieces of paper and those signatures warm our hearts on winter nights. Sign sir, please. Why? Because, as every great sportsman knows, the day to start worrying is when they don't ask you to sign anymore."

CRICKET WRITER DAVID LEMMON ON COLLECTING CRICKET AUTOGRAPHS

TRUEMAN'S BOUNDARY PATROL

WHEN YORKSHIRE fast-bowling legend Freddie Trueman was a teenager, he was called up for National Service as were all young men of the immediate post-war era. Expected to turn out for the Combined Services representative XI, he was given few favours, even though he had recently broken through to the England Test team. Told he couldn't field in his favoured position, leg slip, he huffed off to the boundary. When the Major who'd been given precedence by rank missed a catch in that position, Fred appeared to be in no hurry to prevent the boundary that followed.

At the end of the over, his captain called him over, apoplectic with rage. "What do you think you're doing, Trueman? You'll never play for Combined Services again!" "Too right," smiled the Yorkshireman, "I leave the RAF tomorrow!"

Left arm round...
err over...
err somewhere.

A SIGN OF STARDOM

WHEN A SCHOOLBOY, commentator-to-be Brian Johnston's hero was batsman Patsy Hendren. Finding his idol's address in the newspaper (in an advert for tonic wine), he wrote for his autograph and received no fewer than three back. All had an uncrossed 't' and two lines under the final 'n' – which had such an effect on the impressionable youngster that right into adulthood he still signed his name Johnston with an uncrossed 't' and two final squiggles!

Yes it does, but look how much they paid me to wear it!

GOLDEN GREATS

STRIKING INTRODUCTION

DERBYSHIRE AND ENGLAND 'quickie' Bill Copson would never have thought of taking up cricket at all, let alone for a living, but for the 1926 General Strike. A group of miners decided to play a series of games at a local playing field and Copson, then 17, was encouraged to join in. "I've never had a cricket ball in my hand in my life," he complained – but a friend suggested it would pass the time. His first ball spread-eagled the wicket and, despite allegations of beginner's luck, he continued to do so.

His wit was legendary. At one game, as he trudged up from third man to start a stint (back trouble having given him a stoop), Denis Smith cracked: "Bill, tha walks like Groucho Marx." The reply was immediate. "Ay, and sometimes tha bats like him!" Another time he came to the wicket and put his bat down in the block hole. Declining the umpire's offer of guard, he explained: "I had one here last year." (Not surprisingly, his career batting average was 6.8.)

VILLAGERS TWO COCKY

Village cricket players have always been boastful types – but the men of the Isle of Oxney on the borders of Kent and Sussex met their match in 1830. A local landlord challenged them to an 11 against 2 match to prove they were as good as they claimed they were. The villagers accepted with alacrity – but the two players selected were Kent professionals Edward Wenman and Richard Mills who beat the village XI by 66 runs.

The match was replayed in 1936, with Bill Ashdown (Kent) and Bert Wemsley (Sussex) taking on the Isle of Oxney. As before, the game was a two-innings affair, but only one was played due to the weather after which the professionals had amassed 186 to their more numerous rivals' 153.

WHO WAS WISDEN?

JOHN WISDEN, the man who gave his name to the long-running *Cricketer's Almanack* first published in 1864, had made his own mark fourteen years earlier when he took all ten wickets in a North v South match at Lord's – all clean bowled.

Sir Spencer Ponsonby-Fane described him as "Small of stature but well-made. He bowled moderately fast and was as fair a round-arm bowler as could be seen. The best balls he bowled broke back slightly and his style of delivery tended to make them shoot."

WANT TO GET AHEAD?

BACK IN THE old days, Keith Miller and Denis Compton were pressed into service to advertise Brylcreem. Compton, guided by one of cricket's first agents, accountant Bagenal Harvey, won a then-lucrative advertising contract and became known as the Brylcreem Boy. In 1996, Pakistan Test captain Wasim Akram was fulsome in his praise of a rather more exotic brand of hair care.

"When I am playing test cricket," he revealed, "foaming pomade is the most important thing I take with me everywhere. I have very thick, curly hair which I don't like and this keeps my curls as smooth as a cricket ball. Apart from wanting to look like Clark Gable, I need to keep my hair away from my eyes, especially when bowling, and feel that gel is much more macho than a hair-band."

6 This fellow is the most over-rated player I have ever seen. He looks too heavy, and the way he's been bowling out here, he wouldn't burst a paper bag. 9

HAROLD LARWOOD
ON IAN BOTHAM

6 He has put more backsides on seats than any other English player. 9

BOB TAYLOR
ON IAN BOTHAM

Atherton and Smith on hearing that Allan Donald is being taken off.

Men In The Middle

Dickie By The Book

THE TITLE OF Dickie Bird's forthcoming autobiography was the subject of much speculation. Newspaper readers, invited to put forward suggestions, came up with over 1,000 ideas, which winged their way (so to speak) from as far afield as Australia, Malta and — by fax — Nepal.

Over 40 per cent of respondents came up with A Bird's Eye View, while the more unusual included Views From The Dickie Seat, The Bat Man Cometh and Bird Droppings. Another suggestion: The Umpire Strikes Back!

Bird's Bad Bet

FRESH FROM HIS retirement from international cricket, Dickie Bird began a new career at Windsor in July 1996. It wasn't the umpire we know and love, though, but his two year old namesake — a horse. Unfortunately it struggled in last of seven, the *Sporting Life* commenting it was "slowly away, always struggling in the rear".

Bird Gets Caged

HAROLD 'DICKIE' BIRD was a nervous opening batsmen for Yorkshire and Leicestershire. While with the latter, he prepared to face Lancashire who, at the time, had a couple of quick opening bowlers. When the Leicestershire captain went out to toss, Dickie was seen to disappear into the lavatory. When the skipper came back Dickie, from the security of the lavatory, yelled "Have we won the toss captain?"

"Aye, we have Dickie," replied the captain.

"What are we doing?," asked Dickie.

"We're batting, Dickie lad — get your pads on."

"Oh, Christ !" said Dickie — who shut the door and didn't come out for another ten minutes.

Jail Bird

DICKIE BIRD'S attention to detail is legendary, and often runs to arriving at his venue hours in advance of the start of play. This nearly led him to become the first umpire ever to be arrested when policemen found him trying to scale the walls of the Oval long before the ground had even opened its gates.

Caught In Two Minds

"TITMUS WAS COMPLETELY bemused by the umpire's decision in an up-country match. He got one batsman in so much of a tangle that the ball went off the pads and into the hands of silly point. 'How's that!' snapped Titmus. 'Not out,' said the umpire. 'It hit the bat first.' 'In that case,' replied Titmus 'It must have been a catch.' His suggestion was greeted by a blank stare by the umpire, who was standing in his second first-class match and discovering the hard way that cricket can be very confusing."

JOURNALIST TED CORBETT ON THE PERILS OF BEING AN UMPIRE

HOW ZAT!

Great umpiring Dickie! Here's your Grand.
(Note to Mr Bird's lawyers. This is a joke.)

6 Umpire Dickie Bird is gestating wildly as usual. 9

TONY LEWIS,
BBC-TV

WHITE IS RIGHT

THE UMPIRE'S HABIT of wearing a white coat is thought to have begun in 1861 when batsman the Reverend WG Armitstead complained that he could not see the ball against the dark clothing worn by the umpire at the bowler's end. A white nightshirt was located in the pavilion and the umpire wore this for the remainder of the match between Free Foresters and the United England XI at Eccles, Lancashire.

THE GREAT DIVIDE

IN THE OLDEN days, the distinction between amateurs and professionals — or 'Gentlemen and Players', as they once were termed — was considerable. When on board ship, the two classes would dine at separate tables, while even the way they were portrayed in the press differed until it was abolished in 1963. One particularly funny announcement involved Fred Titmus of Middlesex and England. "In the match card," crackled the tannoy, "for FJ Titmus please read Titmus FJ."

ON GUARD WITH A METAL BLADE

MOUSTACHIO'D AUSTRALIAN quickie Dennis Lillee caused a change in cricket's rules when, in 1979, he came to the wicket in Perth to take guard against England with an aluminium bat. The umpires objected, as did visiting captain Mike Brearley, but all efforts from his own skipper Greg Chappell to change his mind came to nothing. He finally saw reason, apparently flinging the offending bat some 40 yards in his anger. The following week saw the laws of the game changed to specify that the blade of the bat 'shall be made of wood' — and there's never been a repetition.

NAME THAT TUNE!

"WE'RE PLAYING against George Hirst tomorrow," WG Grace advised a young cricketer due to face Yorkshire. "Be sure to bring a box." The abdominal protector, as it's now described, was not as usual an item in the cricketer's wardrobe in the 1890s, but the young man dared not disobey the master. He ventured into Bristol and, entering a sports shop, was faced with a lady sales assistant.

Eventually, he returned with a metal device to do the job, having been told it was the latest 'state of the art' model. The next day he found himself, with his captain at the other end, facing the dangerous Hirst. A couple of well-pitched deliveries preceded one that nipped back off the pitch and caught him amidships... at which his protector let out a tuneful clang.

When this repeated, Grace strode down the wicket and loudly announced: "I said a box, you know — not a musical box."

CALLING MICHAEL FISH...

"THERE'S AN OLD saying in Taunton that if you can see the Quantocks it means rain — if you can't see the Quantocks then it's already raining."

THE LATE, GREAT CRICKET WRITER AND COMMENTATOR JOHN ARLOTT ON BAD WEATHER IN SOMERSET

The cheating
b*s**rds!
They'd tied
the stumps in.

HAPPY WANDERERS

FORMED IN 1845, I Zingari (the name's Italian for 'The Gypsies') is the oldest surviving wandering cricket club. Qualifications for membership were simply for members to be 'not only a good cricketer but a good fellow', while the club's colours of red, black and gold — symbolising an ascent from darkness, through fire, into light, came after their legal adviser Tom Taylor (later editor of *Punch* magazine) returned from Bohemia with some garish gypsy handkerchiefs.

EARLY LUNCHES

UNDERGRADUATES UNDERWHELMED

THERE ARE THOSE who claim that Oxford and Cambridge have no place in first-class cricket. No matter which side of the debate you're on, the fact remains that back in 1877 Oxford University managed to record the worst single-innings score in the first-class game when playing the MCC. They weren't helped, admittedly, by the fact that captain AJ Webbe didn't arrive until after the innings had ended at a total of 12. Only three batsmen made any score at all, while the MCC proved that the pitch wasn't as bad as it seemed by amassing 124.

On the other hand, Oxford's attack was so depleted that the most used bowler, Tylecote (who finished with 8-51) was in fact their wicketkeeper in more usual times! He also opened the innings, but was one of five University men to record 'pairs'. MCC bowled out Oxford in the second innings for 35, winning by an innings and 77 runs. Their bowler Frederick Morley recorded match figures of 13 wickets for 14 runs in 33.1 overs, an astonishing 27 of which were maidens.

BEEFY BANTER

Ian Botham to waiter in Italian restaurant:
"Can you bring me some dolecetti?"

Waiter: **"Don't you mean dolcelatte?"**

Botham: **"That's what I said – dolecetti."**

Waiter: **"No, it's dolcelatte."**

Botham: **"Well, how many Test wickets did you get?"**

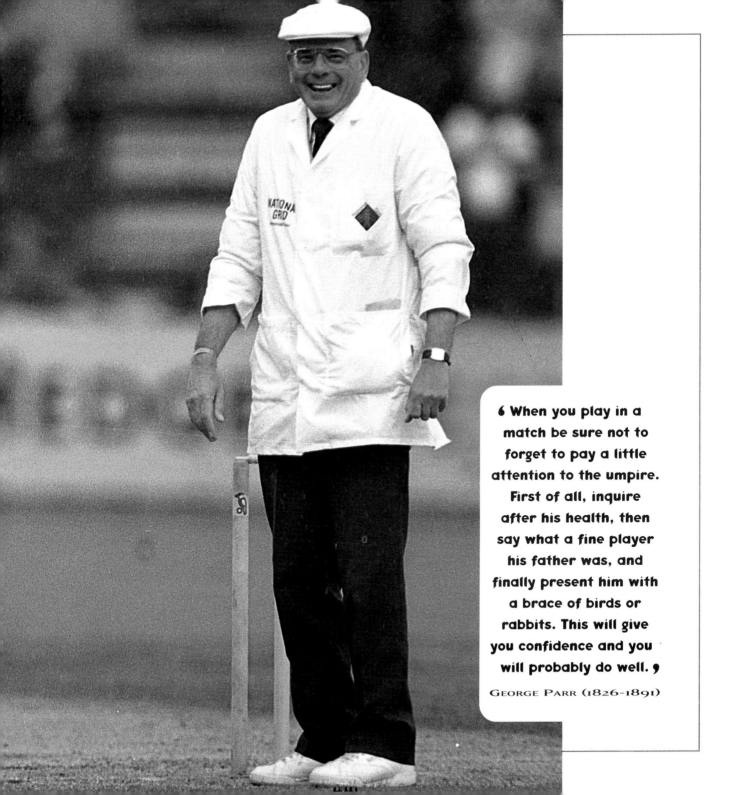

❝ When you play in a match be sure not to forget to pay a little attention to the umpire. First of all, inquire after his health, then say what a fine player his father was, and finally present him with a brace of birds or rabbits. This will give you confidence and you will probably do well. ❞

GEORGE PARR (1826–1891)

OUT OF SIGHT OUT OF MIND

WHILE ON TOUR in Australia, Patsy Hendren and an England team-mate took a car into the outback on a rest day. Idly watching an improvised game of cricket, they were invited to join in. Hendren was waved out into the deep which, because the wicket was high on a hill, was out of sight. There he stood for an hour, enjoying the view and almost oblivious of the shouts and cheers he could hear from a hundred yards' distance.

Eventually after about an hour the clunk of willow on leather was followed by his first sight of the ball coming over the horizon. He held on tight to the catch and advanced over the brow of the hill yelling, "I've caught it! I've caught it!" His captain eyed him with ill-disguised anger. "You silly man," he said (or words to that effect). "We've bowled the other side out... and that's our star batsman you've just dismissed!"

EAT TO WIN

EXTRACT FROM REPORT for the New Zealand Under-19 touring team on 'the pitfalls of eating in Britain: The English breakfast is known for its size. Cereals are passed over for large, often very greasy meals of fried eggs, fried bread, sausages, bacon and Spam. Spam looks and sometimes tastes like dog roll or cat food. However this corned beef is legendary and you may wish to try it as part of your British experience.'

DAVID'S DRINKIES

WHILE TOURING the West Indies, Geoff Boycott spotted David Gower by the side of the swimming pool sipping an exotic cocktail. On enquiring its nature, he was told it was a Pina Colada. He grinned his famous lop-sided grin and pronounced: "No wonder you play like you do. If I drank that bloody stuff, I'd play some daft shots too!"

❝ I always insist my men are in bed by ten o'clock: after all, play starts at half past eleven. ❞

HAMPSHIRE CAPTAIN COLIN INGLEBY-MACKENZIE AFTER THEIR FIRST CHAMPIONSHIP, 1961

INVASION INJURY

THERE HAVE BEEN some strange cricketing injuries in history — but few stranger than the self-inflicted one that Terry Alderman received during the Ashes series of 1982-83. Hoping to quell a pitch invasion when England reached 400 (and doubtless short of patience after a hard and fruitless day in the field) he grabbed one of the intruders and, in the struggle that followed, dislocated his shoulder.

It was re-inserted, but the damage had been done. Not only would he not play any further part in the match but he was also written out of the series.

> **Boycott, being a creature of habit, likes exactly the sort of food he himself prefers.**
>
> DON MOSEY, BBC-TV

If you stretched all the Australian batsmen end to end .... they'd still thrash us.

FOR RICHER, FOR POORER...

"MOST CRICKET WIVES get a pretty rough deal. The summer is spent with festering sacks of rancid jockstraps and sweaty cricket socks, with consorts racing up and down the motorway, playing away half the season, and never at home on weekends. If, for the winter, the accolade of an overseas tour place is bestowed, a wife's joy at the honour and the glory must inevitably be muted by the thought of having to keep the home fires burning. Women stuck at home with young children, while husbands are gadding about in exotic locations, enjoying superstar treatment and the attentions of accommodating groupies may well feel an understandable degree of resentment."

FRANCES EDMONDS (WRITER AND WIFE OF FORMER ENGLAND SPINNER PHIL EDMONDS) ON BEING A CRICKETER'S WIFE...

A WOMAN'S PLACE?

A CERTAIN ENGLAND fast bowler, not being familiar with the customs of foreign parts, was inveigled into taking part in a social tour of the Middle East. A number of friendly games were arranged in the Muslim sheikdom, and during one of these matches the team was invited to a reception given by the local ruler.

The sheik entered the room followed by his harem, and the fast bowler goggled as the procession of women filing past seemed never-ending. He turned to his neighbour and inquired, "Who are all these women?"

"These are the sheik's wives," replied the local informant.

"Good God! How many has he got?" was the next question. "One hundred and ninety nine," came the reply.

"Well," said the fast bowler, "at least he can look forward to something. Another one and he can take the new ball!"

FRANK TYSON, THE CRICKETER WHO LAUGHED

TO WED? NO WAY!

IN THE CASE of breach of promise, £2000 damages were awarded. The only reason the gentleman could give for breaking his engagement was that the lady didn't take any interest in cricket.

LAW REPORT AT THE LIVERPOOL ASSIZES, 1874

ONE BALL LEFT!

"THE BOWLING MACHINE caught him in the unmentionables (Unmentionables, incidentally for all ex-convent schoolgirls, are what we would call 'goolies'). I phoned him when I heard the news on the World Service (you would think they might have more important things to talk about than the state of Edmonds' balls) in order to establish whether the Edmonds lineage was safe. If the worst came to the worst yesterday's Phil could always be tomorrow's Aled Jones. I was relieved to hear his dulcet tones were in the right register. 'Could I inspect his insurance policy,' he wondered, 'and establish whether compensation was payable on a temporarily disabled 'percy'?"

FRANCES EDMONDS TALKING ABOUT HUSBAND PHIL EDMONDS GETTING STRUCK BY A DELIVERY

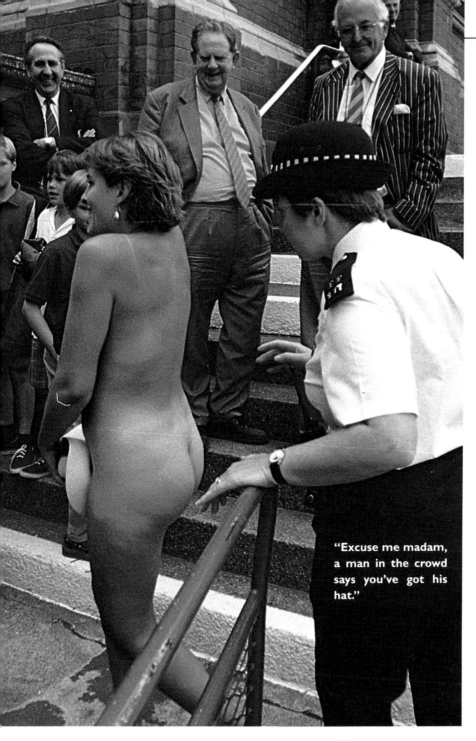

"Excuse me madam, a man in the crowd says you've got his hat."

UMPIRE WALKS TO STAND

UNDAUNTED BY A tube strike, and finding that London's Euston Station didn't serve the south, Leeds umpire Barry Leadbetter walked the two and a half miles across London to reach Waterloo station and continue his journey to a County Championship match at Guildford. He arrived just in time to witness history being made, as fellow umpire Roy Palmer had instructed Cathy Taylor to stand at square leg. Taylor, on duty in the scoreboard, had officiated in the women's Test between England and New Zealand that preceded the Surrey versus Sussex fixture.

LET'S BE WOMEN

THE ATTEMPT OF suffragettes last Thursday to seize a pitch themselves at the Oval, stump oratory being no part of the programme for Hayes' benefit. Anti-suffragists, on the other hand, were allowed to enter and get wet. They were distinguished by brooches bearing the initials LBW (Let's Be Women).

PUNCH, 1908

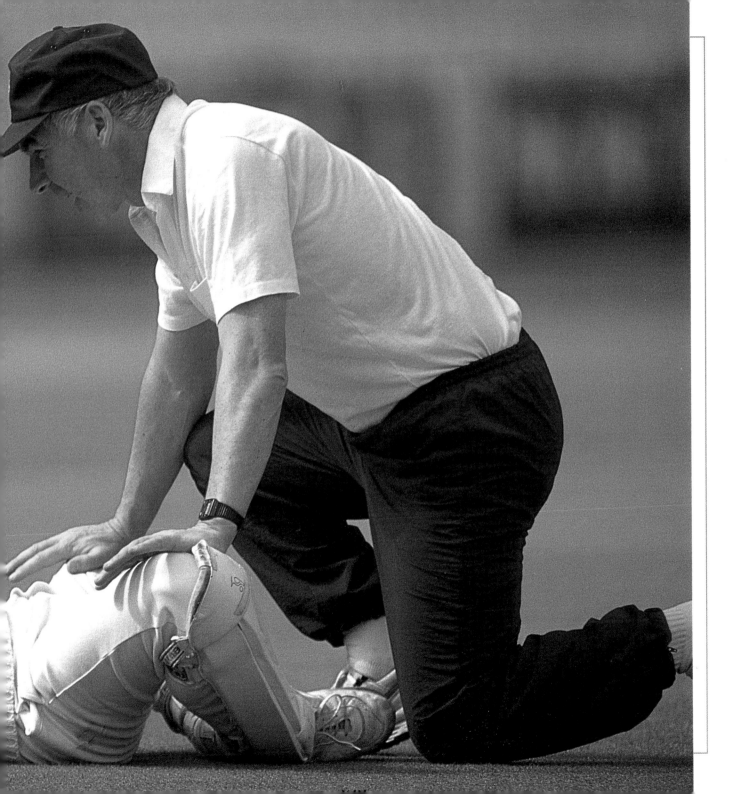

BOGUS BALL BY BALL

IN THE 1930s, when Australian radio was still in its infancy, a commercial broadcasting company devised a plan to broadcast cricket to those too far away from live transmitters. The exercise called for a continuous stream of information to be cabled to a local studio, this being interpreted by the 'commentator' with reference to a plan of the ground, while a 'sound effects' man made the noises of bat and ball to suit the stream of words that was being reconstituted at that end. Such was the lack of sophistication of radio audiences of the time that this was rarely questioned, and a generation grew up believing they had been listening to the 'real thing'!

WISH YOU COULD HEAR!

"ONE OF THE pleasantest parts of the radio commentator's job," said EW Swanton, "was broadcasting good news from Australia to a cold and gloomy England to an audience getting up or having breakfast. In 1950 Freddie Brown's side had been very much up against it in the early State Matches and no-one gave them a chance in the Tests. But on the first day of the First Test at Brisbane they put up a tremendous performance, bowling out Australia on a plumb wicket for 228.

"Golly this will please them at home, I thought, and for ten minutes in the close-of-play summary I let myself go. As I came out of the box, limp and thirsty with the effort, the bored engineer said laconically: 'Suppose ya know we never got through?' The Australian Broadcasting Commission was a more haphazard organisation than it is today..."

6 You can hear the atmosphere. 9

JONATHAN AGNEW,
BBC RADIO

The only change England would propose might be to replace Derek Pringle, who remains troubled by no balls.

THE TIMES

Play has ended here now but they play at Edgbaston until seven, so over there now for some more balls from Rex Alston.

BRIAN JOHNSTON, BBC-TV

The first time you face up to a googly, you're going to be in trouble if you haven't faced up to one before.

TREVOR BAILEY, BBC RADIO

The Centenary Test is unique – a repeat of Melbourne 1977.

JIM LAKER, BBC-TV

NEW-FANGLED FENDER

ALL CRICKET COPY for the newspapers between the wars was handwritten, and such new-fangled appliances as the typewriter were rarely seen. Other scribes, reported EW Swanton, "took it extremely amiss when PGH Fender arrived armed with one at a Test at Old Trafford in the 1930s. I think his was the first typewriter to appear in a cricket press box — and he was promptly relegated to the annexe!"

WHO TURNED OUT THE LIGHTS?

"I WAS DOING an in-vision television summary at Trent Bridge," EW Swanton remembered. "The new electric scoreboard had just been installed, in which the figures were picked out by light bulbs. I said my piece, concluding with the words: 'Now let me just repeat the score, England are...' But when I glanced over to the board to give the total, nothing showed. They had switched off the lights. Brian Johnston told me my expression at that moment was worth a lot. I was completely thrown, having foolishly relied on the board I had not jotted the score down. So I had to make a shot at it and luckily (I believe) got it right."

> **❛ There must be something on Gooch's mind, and he wants to get it off his chest. ❜**
>
> FAROKH ENGINEER,
> BBC-TV

TOO CLOSE TO CALL

LIKE ALL CRICKET'S greatest commentators, veteran Australian Alan McGilvray prided himself on his timing — but came unstuck on one celebrated occasion in December 1960. At Brisbane, the Test Match between Australia and the West Indies seemed certain to be heading for a win for the visitors. Anxious to return to Sydney, McGilvray organised his period of commentary so as to be able to make an early getaway.

On completing his stint and arriving at Sydney Airport, he discovered to his chagrin that the 500th Test had, in fact, ended in a nail-biting tie — a commentator's dream which he forever would regret missing out on!

> **❛ in the back of Merv Hughes' mind must be the feeling that he will dance down the piss and mitch one. ❜**
>
> TONY GREIG, CHANNEL 9 TV

> **❛ Of ian Botham's innings yesterday, soon said least mended. ❜**
>
> JACK BANNISTER,
> TV BBC CRICKET

FROM COMMENTARY TO WITNESS BOX

THE IMRAN-BOTHAM-LAMB libel case in July 1996 saw a constant flow of commuters from the commentary box at Lord's to the High Court in the Strand. Geoff Boycott, muttering, "I'm not going to let them control my life!", was first to be summoned — the moment he set foot at HQ. He was followed by Christopher Martin-Jenkins and former England captain, now TV anchorman, Tony Lewis. Fortunately for all concerned, the current England skipper Mike Atherton had already said his piece the day before. Chairman of selectors Ray Illingworth could afford to see the funny side. "The BBC are so short of commentators," he chuckled, "they've offered me a day's work!"

SWANTON MISSES HIS QUEUE

YOUNG REPORTER EW Swanton, still wet behind the ears, was privileged enough to be at Leyton in 1932 when Yorkshire's legendary partnership of Holmes and Sutcliffe clocked up a record first-wicket stand of 555, beating the record set in 1898 by fellow Yorkshiremen Brown and Tunnicliffe. The story was a hot one, but there was only one telephone – a public one at that – and Swanton, then reporting for the *London Evening Standard*, found himself fourth to last in the queue.

He missed the edition, and was to pay the price when tennis correspondent Sam Harris won the vote to follow England to Australia. "At the time," recalled Swanton, "I was told that Harris's greater news experience had determined the decision, but some years later I heard that the choice had been switched because of the episode at Leyton. 'If he can't get us the story from the East End,' went the reasoning, 'What will he do at Melbourne and Sydney?'"

And this is an essential bit of kit for an England skipper.

RECORD BREAKERS

HADLEE'S HOODOO

JIM LAKER'S RECORD Test wickets haul of all ten in an innings, established in 1956, was all but broken in 1975 by Richard Hadlee. The New Zealand all-rounder, later knighted, finished with 9-52, but was himself the author of his ow misfortune. Had he missed a skied catch from Geoff Lawson off the bowling of Vaughan Brown when the score was 179-8, he'd have had the chance of claiming the final two wickets. As it was he took the catch, and the last wicket to fall, but remained one tantalising dismissal away from the history books.

THOMSON'S TROUBLES

THE HEADLINES MADE by the 1974-75 Ashes series in Australia belonged to one man and one man only. Jeff Thomson, the junior partner to Dennis Lillee in most cases, was out on his own in terms of unplayability, and when he wrapped up England's first innings in the Fifth Test with what was incredibly his 33rd wicket of the series so far, all the signs pointed to his breaking Arthur Mailey's record – set as far back as 1920-21 – of 36.

When the second innings started, the ground was in a high state of expectation. Unfortunately Jeff Thomson wasn't. On the rest day preceding it, he'd played a game of tennis and managed to tear shoulder muscles while doing so. While he was able to field, he most certainly wasn't going to bowl. It was doubtless little consolation that quickie rival Rodney Hogg broke the record four years later. Moral: don't mix your sports!

❛ To be a great fast bowler you need a big heart and a big bottom. ❜

FRED TRUEMAN

❛ I am not saying that it is necessary for a fast bowler to be a homicidal maniac, but it certainly helps. ❜

MICHAEL PARKINSON

ONE MAN, TWO HAT-TRICKS

A TRIANGULAR TOURNAMENT played in Manchester in 1912 between England, South Africa and Australia gave the latter's leg-spin bowler Jimmy Matthews the chance to make history by registering two hat-tricks in a day. Both were against South Africa, following on after Australia's opening innings of 448.

Returning to the attack with South Africa 265-7, Matthews bowled his first victim then took the second and third leg-before.

Having polished off the tail, it wasn't too long before he returned to the attack when the Springboks followed on. His first victim was bowled, the second caught and bowled. Fascinatingly it was the same player, Ward – the tail-ender promoted – who faced the hat-trick ball second time around. The ball dollied into the air and it was Matthews himself who caught it, completing a record haul which, interestingly, had been achieved without the help of a single fielder.

'TON' FOR TWO

PERCY FENDER'S whirlwind century, scored in 35 minutes for Surrey against Northamptonshire in 1920, remained an unchallenged record for over 60 years. Technically it was equalled by Lancashire batsman Steve O'Shaughnessy whose 'ton' was scored in 54 balls, at least eight more than Fender.

The achievement was considerably cheapened by the fact that, in a rain-affected end-of-season game Leicester were trying to 'buy' a declaration in the hope of winning through to third place in the County Championship table. Nevertheless, the *Manchester Evening News* introduced the two record holders to one another, Fender then being a venerable 91 not out.

THE DON'S MASTER CLASS

AUSTRALIA'S DON BRADMAN is the only Test player to have exceeded the 300 mark twice. His record could have been even better had he not run out of partners while playing against South Africa in 1932. His first innings in the Fourth Test saw him amassing runs steadily but losing players at the other end. Hugh Thurlow was eleventh and last on the team sheet, but was run out – many claim the Don was at fault with a late "get back" call – leaving his partner marooned on 299 not out. The match was won by ten wickets, offering no chance of amends in a series which had already brought him three single hundreds.

TAYLOR-MADE — EVENTUALLY

BOB TAYLOR, THE England and Derbyshire wicketkeeper, was approaching JT Murray's record of first-class victims as an England tour of Australia loomed. Finally, he equalled the 1,527 mark and was expected to beat it in the opening match of the tour against Queensland in Brisbane. His teammates steeled themselves for a mass celebration...but all seemed in vain.

Three times in the first innings Taylor raised the ball aloft in confident anticipation of a 'caught behind' decision... and three times he was denied. Amazingly, he claimed not a single victim in the first innings, and it was only in Queensland's second spell at the wicket that he established a new record – with a stumping!

AWOL:
ALIAS WAS OUT AT LEICESTERSHIRE

BEFORE WORLD WAR I it was common for county cricketers to use aliases so as to keep their real identity from the newspapers, either for the purposes of privacy or because they were undergraduates who were supposed to be at university.

The most famous example was the captain of the Canadian side that toured England in 1880. Halfway through the tour his real identity was revealed and he was discovered to be a deserter from the English army. He was arrested during a match with Leicestershire and was sent to prison.

TOO LATE TO BAT

DENIS COMPTON was driving across Vauxhall Bridge on his way to the last day's play in the Oval Test. It was just 11am and Denis was running late as usual. He switched on the car radio, for a time check, only to hear John Arlott saying, "Well, now that Bill Edrich is out we'll be seeing Denis Compton next." He was wrong. In his light-hearted way, our Denis had forgotten that on the last day play starts half an hour earlier.

KEN BARRINGTON

‘ I bowled
bouncers for
one reason, and
that was to hit
the batsman
and thus
intimidate him. ’

DENNIS LILLEE

THE SHOT THAT LOST THE CUP

AT 132-2 IN the 1987 World Cup Final, England looked a good bet to win for the first ever time. Bill Athey and Mike Gatting were well set, with the captain setting about the opposition, bowling with gusto. At his wits' end the Australian captain put himself on to bowl, whereupon Gatting played the shot that, some still argue, lost the Cup.

It was the reverse sweep, a stroke fraught with danger which had cost him his wicket in the semi-final when he'd played on. On this occasion, a top edge deflected off his shoulder to provide stumper Greg Dyer with a relatively simple chance. England failed to hit the target by the narrowest of margins, just seven runs being needed. England have yet to win the World Cup...

BOTHAM AND BOB BOUNCE BACK

WHO'D BET ON a team faced with following on 227 runs behind against mighty Australia? Only once in Test history had a side following on managed to win, but England made it two in July 1981 at Headingley. They'd gathered just 174 in reply to the visitors' 401-9 declared, and languished on 135-7 before Ian Botham and Graham Dilley added 117 runs as part of 216 added in just 35 overs. The hero of the hour inevitably, was Botham, playing with a bat borrowed from Graham Gooch. His 149 brought the match to a fifth day — surprising his team-mates who'd booked out of their hotel assuming the game was all but over. Australia were reduced from 56-1 to 75-8, largely thanks to the rejuvenated Bob Willis and were all out for 111.

AN ARRESTING PERFORMANCE

WHEN BIG-HITTING Clive Lloyd arrived at one of Kent's smaller grounds, and with the home attack not at its most potent, his usually wide smile became wider. The ball began departing the ground at regular intervals and a local old lady, watching slates bounce off her roof, put in a call to the constabulary. A sergeant then arrived in a Panda car and, not being familiar with the cricket ground, made the press box his first call. "Hello, hello — what's going on then?" quoth the man in blue. The Kent 12th man, who was visiting the box at the time, looked up and responded. "Glad you're here, sergeant. It's that man out there. I think you should lock him up before he does any more damage."

JUST THE TICKET

IN 1995 A certain CN Evans, playing for the Maghoraland Select XI against Northamptonshire returned from the crease one afternoon with his score on four since he was obliged to attend a court hearing for a traffic offence. Fortunately his team batted till close of play and he returned the next day — doubtless making sure he parked well away from any yellow lines!

> **' Welcome to Leicester, where the captain Ray illingworth has just relieved himself at the Pavilion End. '**
>
> BRIAN JOHNSTON, BBC RADIO

GOOCH SLIPS AWAY

IN THE LATE June of 1996, the TCCB announced a special dispensation to Law 2, Section 8 for former England captain Graham Gooch. Gooch, recently voted onto the national selection panel, was allowed to leave the game between Essex and Surrey early because he was scheduled to help his fellow selectors pick the England team for the forthcoming Third Test between England and India.

WRONG WAY DAVE

WHEN DAVID STEELE gained his first England cap in 1975 at the advanced age of 34, he was so used to coming out at Lords while playing for his county side, Northants, from the visitors dressing room that he got completely lost! When called to the wicket with England already 10-1, he ended up in the toilet after taking a series of wrong turns! Happily the story had a happy ending: he made a half-century and topped the England averages that summer.

If I find the joker with the superglue...

THE LONGEST INNINGS

BEFORE THE DAYS of motor cars, a commercial traveller found himself at a lonely railway station in the north of Scotland which was manned by a station-master and a porter.

Told he would have to wait four hours for the next train, he enquired of the porter if there were any places of interest nearby — a cinema, castle, stately home or garden — where he might amuse himself. The porter said there was nothing, but perhaps the traveller would care to join him and the station master in a game of cricket, their own way of passing the time? The station master took the bat and the traveller was put on to bowl, with the porter as fielder. The first ball removed the station master's middle stump, and the porter went into extended celebrations which the traveller thought somewhat excessive.

Asking why the porter was so pleased, he received this reply. "You would be, too — you see, he's been in for four years!"

HANDS TOGETHER

ENGLAND'S LEGENDARY cricketing vicar, David Sheppard won a surprise recall to the national team for their 1962-63 winter tour to Australia. He was, however, short on match practice and after a torrid time in the slips was exhorted to "pretend it's Sunday and keep your hands together" by an irate Freddie Trueman.

Worse, however, was to come. He made considerable ground round the boundary to take a catch from Australia's captain Bill Lawry. Unfortunately, back at the wicket the umpire was signalling a no ball. Once the unfortunate Sheppard had retrieved the ball, having thrown it in the air in time-honoured celebratory fashion, he found the batsmen had stolen an extra run!

MAX-IMUM EXTRAS

DURING THE 1975 Ashes series in England the visiting bowler Max Walker chased a well-hit shot towards the boundary. Flinging himself at the ball, he succeeded in stopping it crossing the rope for four runs, but overshot and had to scramble back. By the time he'd regained his balance and thrown in, the batsmen had run five.

BEEFY BANTER (2)

BOTHAM TO SIMON HUGHES: "Cor, Yozzer, you aren't half scruffy."

Hughes: "Listen Beefy, if I earned a third of what you earn I'd be able to afford some decent clothes."

Botham: "If you earned a third of what I earned you'd be a tax exile."

THE OLD ENEMY

DURHAM'S DEFEAT OF Yorkshire in 1973's Gillette Cup was acclaimed by the newspapers as, "A result more improbable than Sunderland's defeat of Leeds in the (same year's) FA Cup Final." The match threw up an interesting clash in brothers Chris and Alan Old who faced each other for the first time in a competitive match: Chris, the England fast bowler, played for Yorkshire while Durham's Alan had also represented his country — but at rugby! However, Durham, who took the match by five wickets with 8.3 overs to spare would have to wait many more seasons to become a first-class county.

"**THERE ARE MOMENTS** playing tennis when I feel like Edberg, and moments when I'm playing golf (though far fewer) when I feel like Ballesteros. Cricket is only an extension of that. There are times – like the evening after scoring a century for instance – that I get the urge to go out and practice eight hours a day so that they will come along more often. This urge, I have to say, disappears almost as quickly as it arrives."

DAVID GOWER

THE LONG AND SHORT

WATCHING TONY GRIEG'S long legs eating up the pitch on the first day of the Test and David Steele's short ones scampering after, I was reminded of Harry Pilling of Lancashire, the shortest cricketer in the first-class game. Asked if he didn't feel at a disadvantage when batting with the giant Clive Lloyd, he replied: "Naw. Not so long as 'e doesn't tread on me."

PUNCH, 1975

A good Captain should be able to handle the press.

THANKS, BUT NO THANKS

THE CAPTAINCY OF any county is an honour accorded to few: to captain Yorkshire, especially with its (until recently) stringent qualifications, must be even more of a prize. Yet in 1928 the legendary Herbert Sutcliffe actually declined the offer sent to him while he was touring South Africa with the England team. Short, sharp and to the point (as most Yorkshiremen are), his response read:

"Official invitation received yesterday. Many thanks to you and your committee. Great honour. Regret to decline. Willing to play under any captain selected."

The man to whom he responded, county President Lord Hawke, had been a pre-war captain who'd imposed a draconian discipline on his men who, as well as being sober and well dressed, had to be clean shaven, moustaches apart. "If I shave twice a day," he remarked, "the least you can do is shave once."

CRICKETING EVOLUTION

WHEN MAN FIRST arose from the primitive ape,
He first dropped the tail, and took on a new shape
But cricketing man, born to trundle and swipe
reversion displays to the earlier type
For a cricketing team, when beginning to fail,
Always loses its 'form' and develops a 'tail'!

PUNCH, 1892

A LORDLY PROGRESS

WE HAVE PLAYED the Eton and were most confoundedly beat: however, it was some comfort to me that I got eleven notches in the first inning and seven in the second, which was more than any of our side except Brockman and Ipswich could contrive to hit.

After the match we dined together, and were extremely friendly; not a single discordant word was uttered by either party. To be sure, we were most of us rather drunk, and went home together to the Haymarket where we kicked up a row... How I got home after the play, God knows.

HARROW SCHOOLBOY LORD BYRON, 1805

THE NAME GAME

FORMER DERBYSHIRE wicket-keeper Bob Taylor is such a devotee of the game that he named his house 'Hambledon' in recognition of the village where it all started. Not that this impressed his county colleagues. Asked where Taylor lived, one replied: "I can tell you where it is, but don't ask the address. It's a house with a funny name."

❛ Byron played in the Eleven, and very badly too. He should never have been in the Eleven had my counsel been taken. ❜

HARROW CAPTAIN
CHARLES LLOYD, 1808

HOW
ZAT

BLIND EYE AT LONG LEG

"BEING A DEAF cricketer has its benefits as well as drawbacks. I have to concentrate on looking at the other batsmen when we're running because I can't hear them. I've run loads of colleagues out. I have to constantly keep an eye on the captain for field changes. On the other hand, if I'm bowling a hard spell, and I'm fielding in the deep I can just look the other way or pretend I haven't heard, and they'll let me have a rest in the outfield."

ANDREW POLLOCK, SON OF SOUTH AFRICAN STAR GRAEME POLLOCK

UNDERARM DELIVERY

WITH THE 'BEST OF FIVE' World Series Final of 1981 standing at one game apiece between Australia and New Zealand, much hung on the result of the third which might put one of the countries in the box seat. When New Zealand were set 235 to beat, a solid stand between openers Wright and Edgar put them in immediate contention.

At the start of the final over the Kiwis were 221-6 and needed 15 to win – far from impossible with doughty all-rounder Richard Hadlee at the crease. He hit the first ball from Trevor Chappell, brother of Australian captain Ian, for four, but was out leg before by the next delivery. Ian Smith, the next man in, hit two twos, but was then bowled, leaving new batsman Brian McKechnie to face the sixth and final ball.

Only a six could tie the match and force a replay – but that unlikely scenario was rendered even more of an outside chance when Ian Chappell instructed his brother to bowl this delivery underarm. This was within the rules of the Australian game, until outlawed the following week as the Australian Cricket Board 'deplored' their captain's action. Nevertheless, two days later Chappell was voted Man of the Series as his side took an unassailable 3-1 lead.

HOW
ZAT!

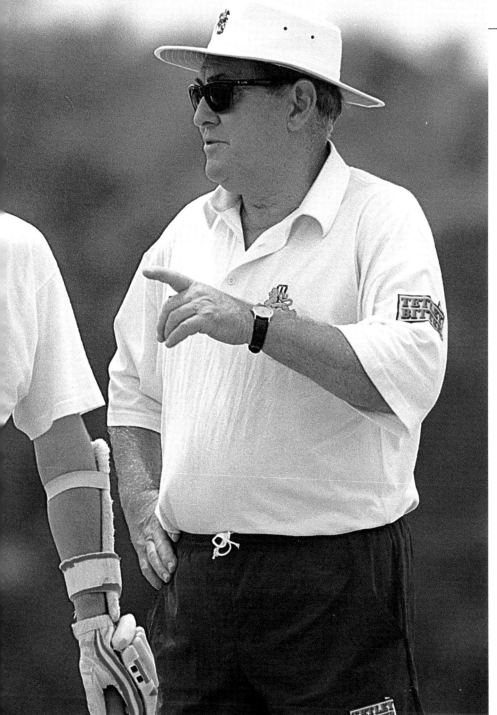

Mike Atherton, wearing padding on his forearm, both thighs and over his kidneys, watches as chairman of selectors Ray Illingworth models Puma's new stomach pad.

FIELDER CATCHES A... BUS

WHILE PLAYING FOR Ilfracombe against Woolacombe on a hilltop ground at Hele, north Devon, in 1996, fielder Paul Crabb ended up returning to the ground via bus after the ball had flown over not only the boundary rope but also a hedge. It rolled down the steep hill towards Hele village with Crabb in hot pursuit. After a chase of a quarter of a mile, he elected to invest 21p in a bus ticket for the return journey.

THE PHOTOGRAPHERS